The Ashford Book of
TEXTURES & TOWELS
for the FOUR SHAFT LOOM

ELSA KROGH has written several books on spinning and weaving. This book was first published in 1994, with a second edition in 1997, and it has been translated into English (with a few alterations) for publication by Ashford Handicrafts, New Zealand.

Elsa bought her first Ashford spinning wheel after living in New Zealand from 1966 to 1970. She began importing them into Denmark soon after and has been the Danish distributor for Ashford Handicrafts ever since.

Elsa finds weaving an absorbing hobby with challenges to both the hands and the mind. She started on the rigid heddle loom, which she still uses, and went on to shaft looms. She has one four-shaft loom and two eight-shaft looms, but prefers the four-shaft techniques as they allow more variations and possibilities than most weavers realise. She also likes to weave inkle bands.

The Ashford Book of
TEXTURES & TOWELS
for the FOUR SHAFT LOOM

Elsa Krogh

Ashford Handicrafts

First published in Denmark in 1997

This edition published in 2002 by
Ashford Handicrafts Ltd
415 West Street, Ashburton, New Zealand
in association with
Shoal Bay Press Ltd
Box 17661, Christchurch, New Zealand

ISBN 1 877251 15 1

Printed by Rainbow Print Ltd, Christchurch, New Zealand

CONTENTS

Ashford Table Loom

Weaving widths: 40cm, 60cm, 80cm (16in, 24in, 32in).

Choose from four or eight shafts.

Kit includes:

    Stainless steel reed 40/10 – 10dpi

    Texsolv heddles

    Two shuttles

Ashford Jack Loom

Weaving widths: 97cm, 115cm (38in, 45in).

Choose from four or eight shafts

Kit includes:

    Stainless steel reed 40/10 – 10dpi

    Texsolv heddles

    Two ski shuttles

INTRODUCTION

About Towels

Towels are wonderful projects for the loom. You can weave small fingertip towels or large bath towels, thin dishtowels for the kitchen or bulky towels for the bathroom. They are all useful, and they make excellent gifts, if you have friends or family members with an interest in cooking or an eye for colour-coordinated bathrooms.

And when you have chosen the type to weave, and put the warp on the loom, you don't have to make them all the same, so it is an obvious way to use up odds and ends of nice yarns and gorgeous colours, if the yarn is suitable for the purpose.

For beginners it is a consolation that a towel will do its job even if the weaving is slightly irregular and the edges not quite straight. Use a series of towels as an exercise in weaving yardage or weaving several pieces exactly or almost the same size. For advanced weavers it is an excellent way to test unusual colour combinations, new yarns, and interesting techniques.

A towel warp can be used for more than towels. The width and the materials are also suitable for placemats, cushions, and bags. The narrow width makes towel weaving ideal for narrow looms.

Materials

The yarns used for warp and weft must of course be able to absorb moisture. This means using linen, cotton, cotton-linen blends, ramie, and a few other vegetable fibres. They are designed by nature to transport moisture: just what we need. Unbleached natural fibres, especially cotton, may require a couple of washings before they can function properly.

Substitutions and sampling

If you haven't got or can't get the yarn specified in the instructions, please don't hesitate to use what you have or can get. The sett needs to be adjusted, of course, if the yarn is thinner or thicker, and this will make the towel narrower or wider than the original, but does it matter? Only take care to weave it correspondingly shorter or longer. You will get a useable product, perhaps better than the original.

Always put on some extra warp for sampling. It is important to check for threading errors, and to see if the sett is right. Weave a fair sized sample and wash it, so you can see how much it will shrink, and how it will feel and look. If you don't like it, now is the time to change sett or weft material.

Techniques

Any technique can be used, as long as it results in a stable and supple product which can absorb moisture and survive daily use and modern washing machines. Plain weave and twill are excellent, but slightly textural weaves such as huckaback and waffle catch the moisture better, because of the uneven surface. Some of the techniques used in the towels here would be suitable for other projects, such as scarves in fine wool or silk.

Finishing

- Machine zigzag each end of the woven length. If it is very long, you can divide it into shorter pieces to make it more manageable.
- Soak the fabric in a warm, mild detergent solution for 1 hour. Watch out for running colours.
- Wash it again in the washing machine in warm water on a regular cycle. The preliminary soaking should prevent unsightly, permanent creases, which can form if the fabric is put into the washing machine directly from the loom.
- Hang the woven length up until it is almost dry, then press it with a steam iron. If you have access to a cold mangle, please do use this for the towels with linen weft. They will look wonderful.
- Cut the towels apart. Fold the hem and stitch by hand or machine. All my towels have a hanger – a short piece of inkle band – at one end, often sewn into the fold. The band is woven on an inkle loom with warp or weft yarn left over from the project.
- Press the towels again, and they are ready for use.

Floating Selvage

The first and the last warp ends go through the reed as usual, but are not drawn through the heddles. They go directly from front beam to back beam, and always form a horizontal line at the edges of the warp, while the rest of the warp ends go up and down, making the shed. At each pick the shuttle goes into the shed over, and comes out under the floating selvage. This way all wefts are tied down at the edge, irrespective of technique.

When the floating selvages begin to feel slack, hang some kind of weight on them at the back of the loom by means of a smooth hook or similar.

Table of Approximate Running Lengths

Cotton 8/2:	6,400 m/kg	3,200 yds/lb
Cotton 10/2:	8,500 m/kg	4,220 yds/lb
Cotton 12/2:	10,000 m/kg	5,000 yds/lb
Cotton 16/2:	13,000 m/kg	6,500 yds/lb
Cotton 20/2:	17,000 m/kg	8,500 yds/lb
Tow 6/1:	3,600 m/kg	1,800 yds/lb
Linen 8/1:	4,800 m/kg	2,400 yds/lb
Linen 16/1:	9,600 m/kg	4,800 yds/lb
Cottolin 22/2:	6,400 m/kg	3,200 yds/lb

Warp Calculations

Length of warp

Length of 1 towel x no. of towels
(remember extra for hem)   _____

Take up (depending on weave,
but at least 10%)   _____

Shrinkage (at least 10%, more if
the yarn is unbleached cotton)   _____

Loom waste (tying on and thrumms)   _____

Samples (plus new tying on)   _____

Total length of warp   _____

Width of warp

Finished width   _____

Take up (approx. 10%,
depending on weave and material)   _____

Shrinkage of weft
(depending on weave and material)   _____

Width in reed   _____

Number of warp ends = Sett (No of ends per cm (inch)) x width in reed.

Amount of material

No of warp ends x length of warp (in metres (yards)):   _____ (A)

Running length of warp yarn   _____ (B)

Divide A by B to get amount $\dfrac{A}{B}$ =   _____
(in kilos (pounds)) of the warp yarn:

How to Read the Instructions

Technique = name of weaving technique.

Finished size = length x width, measured on the finished article. (This information may appear later on the list, if there is more than one size woven on the same warp.)

Warp = material and type; amount used per towel. *

Sett = how many ends per cm (inch).

Width in reed = cm (inches).

No of ends = sett x width.

Warping order = if more than one colour in the warp.

Weft = material and type; amount used per towel. *

Weaving = pattern or colour repeats, picks per cm (inch). Any measurements are taken on the tensioned warp.

Remarks = suggestions and comments.

Drawdown

• The threading is shown at the bottom and begins at the right side, progressing towards the left.
• The tie-up is for rising shaft looms (sinking shaft looms, see below **).
• The treadling begins just above the tie-up and progresses upwards, just like the weaving itself.
• OBS: There are two tie-ups and treadlings. The left one, next to the interlacement diagram, is for the jack loom. The one to the right is for the table loom.
• In the interlacement diagram of the drawdown, the warp is shown as white squares, the weft is shown as grey squares. Any deviation is shown in the bars below the threading and to the right of the treadling.
• Black-and-white drawdowns are profile drafts.

Reeds

The instructions specify how many ends per cm (inch), not which reed to use. I normally thread 2 ends per dent, so the reed will be, for example, 40/10 for 8 ends per cm (10dpi for 20epi). You can also thread 3 or 4 ends per dent or, alternatively, 1 and 2 ends per dent. To find the reed for one of the instructions, divide the number of ends per cm (inch) by 2 (or 3 or 4 or 1.5) to see if you can use a reed you already have. Get as close as you can: it doesn't have to be 100% precise. A reed 48/10 (12 dpi) with 3 ends per dent will be fine for 'Blue and green warp stripes' or 32/10 (8dpi) with 2 ends per dent for 'Winter white waffle'.

* All amounts are approximate and should be taken as a guideline only, as there may be differences between yarns from different manufacturers.

** For sinking shaft looms (counterbalanced and countermarch), use the jack loom tie-up, but the white squares instead of the black ones.

THE TOWELS

1. TWILL – SIMPLE AND STYLISH

A simple twill is not the least bit simple. It is very versatile indeed. A plain 1-2-3-4 threading can be treadled in many ways. The two examples here are both woven in the ordinary 2/2 twill, because it looks good with the warp stripes, and is ideal for the purpose. However, with a plain warp without stripes I might have chosen plain weave or basket weave, or a broken twill, or changed the tie-up to weave 3/1 twill for placemats with a heavy linen weft.

Natural with dotted pinstripes

Technique:	2/2 twill
Finished size:	67 cm x 44.5 cm (26" x 17.5")
Warp:	cotton 10/2, natural, 44 g (1.6 oz), and cotton 8/2, black, 10 g (0.35 oz) per towel.
Sett:	10 ends per cm (24-25 epi)
Width in reed:	48 cm (19")
No of ends:	484 (the first 2 and the last 2 ends double in heddles and reed).

Warping order

Natural:	40	1	1	28	+12
Black:		1	4	1	
		<—	x12	—>	

Wind the warp this way: 41 nat. + (6 bl. + 30 nat.) x 12 + 11 nat. = 484 ends. Let one natural end and one black end change place at the edges of the black stripes when threading.

Weft
Tow 6/1, natural; 100 g per towel.

Weaving
Weave in twill with approx. 8 picks per cm (20 ppi).

Most of the warp was woven in one piece with this weft, and was cut into suitable lengths afterwards, but at the end of the warp I wove a few towels with white linen weft (8/1 and 16/2), with narrow weft stripes of orange 8/1 and pink 16/2 respectively.

Remarks
The 6/1 tow yarn feels stiff and dull and heavy, but just wait. The washing transforms it into a soft and absorbent material with the unmistakable shine of linen.

The rustic look of unbleached tow yarn goes particularly well with pottery mugs and wooden bowls. Make a long warp, and weave placemats on half of it, towels on the other half.

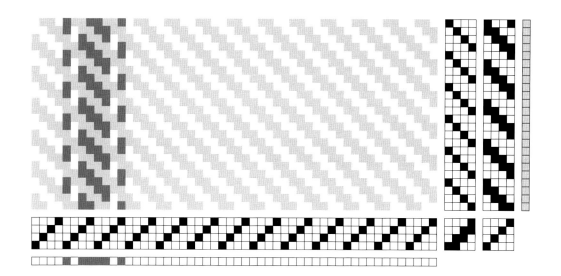

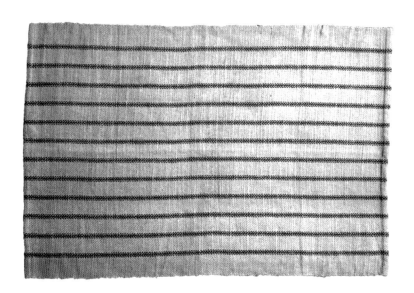

Blue and green warp stripes

Technique:	2/2 twill
Finished size:	81 cm x 46.5 cm (32" x 18").
Warp:	Cotton 16/2, natural, 15 g (0.5" oz), plus 2 blue and 2 green shades, 10 g (0.35 oz) of each, per towel.
Sett:	14 ends per cm (35 epi)
Width in reed:	50 cm (approx. 20")
No. of ends:	704 (the first 4 and the last 4 ends double in heddle and reed = 2 x 2 in each side).

Warping order

Natural	24	8	8	8	16	+ 8
A. blue		32				
B. greenblue			32			
C. green				32		
D. bluegreen					32	
		<—		x 4		—>

Weft

Linen 16/1, white; approx. 75 g (2.6 oz) per towel.

Weaving

The whole length is woven as yardage, as one piece to be cut up afterwards. 14 picks per cm (35 ppi).

Remarks

If you don't want the irregular spacing between the coloured warp stripes, make all the spacings (in natural) 8 ends wide, and *begin* and *end* with 32 ends of natural.

With the regular spacing you can use another colour repeat, such as:

3 colours (A + B + C) x 5 plus an extra A = 16 stripes.

5 colours (A + B + C + D + E) x 3 plus an extra A = 16 stripes.

In both cases you begin and end with 32 warp ends of natural, and with spacings of 8 ends of natural between the 16 coloured stripes.

If you would like to weave separate hems on the twill towels, use plain weave and a finer weft. Only remember to check (by weaving a sample) that the tabby + fine weft don't shrink differently from the twill + main weft.

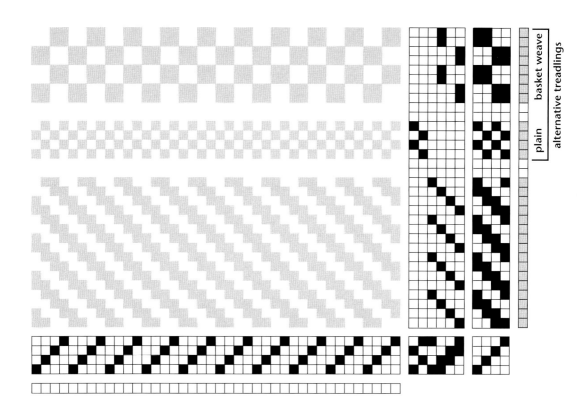

2. WINTER WHITE WAFFLE

Technique:	Waffle weave
Finished size:	103 cm x 52 cm (40" x 20.5")
Warp:	Cotton 8/2, natural; 120 g (4.2 oz) per towel.
Sett:	10 ends per cm (24-25 epi)
Width in reed:	66 cm (26")
No of ends:	656 (the first 2 and the last 2 ends = floating selvage, not shown on drawdown).

Note: this weave uses a varying number of heddles on the shafts – please check and move, if necessary, before starting to thread.

Weft

Cotton 16/2, white and black, used double except in hem; 120 g white (4.2 oz) and 20 g black (0.7 oz) per towel.

Weaving

Weave 5 cm (2") hem with single weft, see drawdown.

Then continue with double weft and full treadling, and 9 picks per cm (22.5 ppi).

20 repeats (each 8 picks) with white.

Border (black weft always begins and ends on the middle treadle):

13 picks of black

11 picks of white

13 picks of black

11 picks of white

37 picks of black

11 picks of white

13 picks of black

11 picks of white

13 picks of black

Weave approx. 60 cm (24") with white weft only.

Repeat border as above, then 20 repeats with white weft. Change to single white weft and weave the hem.

Remarks

The front and the back of the towel are not identical.

It would be easy to tie up a sixth treadle to weave plain weave (for hem), but please do not do this. Waffle weave has a terrible take-up, and a hem in plain weave would flare conspicuously. This is the reason for the mini-waffle weave used in the hem here.

Because of this take-up (in both directions), add at least 30% (take-up plus shrinkage) when planning the warp.

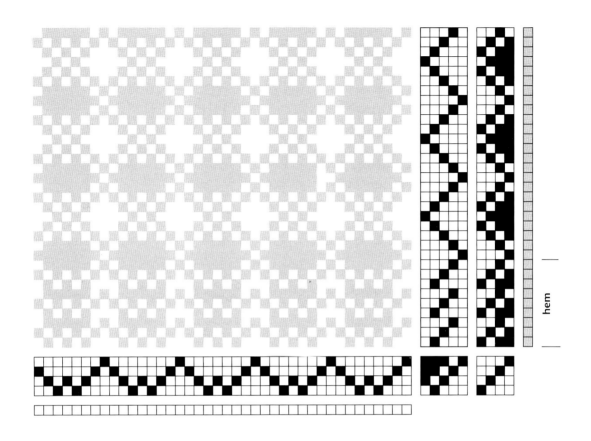

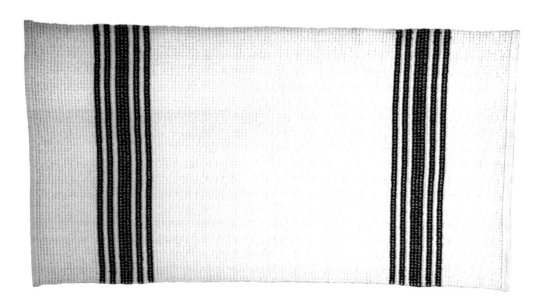

3. THREE TEXTURES SIDE BY SIDE

Inspired by Barbara Smith Eychaner's placemats in *Handwoven* May/June 93.

Technique:	Plain weave, basket weave, and crepe.
Finished size:	See under individual versions.
Warp:	Cotton 8/2, natural + a small amount of coloured 8/2 (pink in linen weft version, blue in cotton weft version). Used double. Amounts, see below.
Sett:	6 double ends per cm (15 double epi).
Width in reed:	58 cm (23").
No of ends:	348 double ends (328 natural + 20 coloured).

Warping order
All ends double.

Natural:	20	18	17	18	16	150	
Coloured:		2	2	2	2	2	Repeat border in opposite order

The warping order looks messy, but don't worry – it is much easier than it looks. Only the 328 natural (double) ends are an ordinary warp, measured out and put on the loom, beamed and threaded through heddles and reed, and tied on to the front warp stick.

At the threading you leave those heddles empty which are intended for the coloured warp ends. These are measured out, stripe by stripe, and threaded from the back of the loom through heddles and reed, and tied on to the front warp stick as a supplementary warp, hanging over the back beam of the loom with a weight attached to each of the stripes.

This way you can change the colour of the warp stripes whenever you feel like it, so the supplementary warp doesn't have to be as long as the main warp. However, it should be so long that it can always hang over the back beam, to keep the warp tensioned.

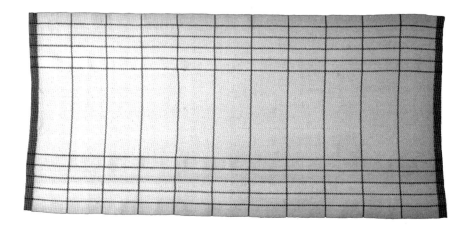

Remarks

Keep the warp as taut as possible, and beat the weft gently in place. Beating hard on a soft warp may compress the basket weave and the crepe more than the plain weave, so the fell gets wavy.

Linen Weft Version

Finished size: 82 cm x 52 cm (32" x 20.5")

Warp: cotton 8/2, natural, 100 g (3.5 oz),
and cotton 8/2, pink, 10 g (0.35 oz).

Weft

linen 16/1, white, 10 g (0.35 oz)
tow 6/1, white, 80 g (2.8 oz)
linen 8/1, orange, 8 g (0.28 oz)

Weaving

5 cm (2") with linen 16/1 for hem,
12.5 cm (5") with tow 6/1, at approx. 9 picks per cm (22.5 ppi),
(4 picks of orange 8/1 + 8 cm (3.1") tow 6/1) x 8, but end with 12.5 cm (5") with tow 6/1, 5 cm (2") with 16/1 for hem.

Cotton Weft Version

Finished size: 110 cm x 52 cm (43" x 20.5")

Warp: cotton 8/2, natural, 120 g (4.2 oz),
and cotton 8/2, blue, 12 g (0.42 oz).

Weft

cottolin 22/2, white, 100 g (3.5 oz)
cottolin 22/2, green, 10 g (0.35 oz)

Weaving

Approx. 9 picks per cm (22.5 ppi).
5 cm (2") green for hem,
(10 cm (4") white + 4 picks of green) x 11,
10 cm (4") white, and 5 cm (2") green.

Remarks

The original was woven with a cotton yarn that is no longer available. I have suggested using cottolin 22/2 instead, as this will result in a better towel, lighter and more absorbent.

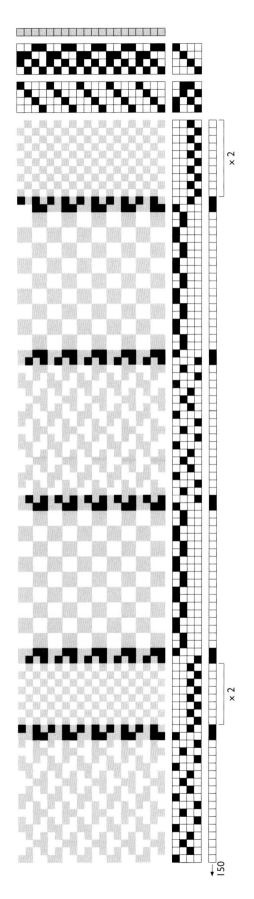

4. THICK AND THIRSTY HUCKABACK

Technique: Huckaback (huck lace).

Finished size: 109 cm x 58 cm (43" x 23").

Warp: Cotton 8/2, natural; approx. 125 g (4.4 oz) per towel.

Sett: 8 ends per cm (20 epi).

Width in reed: 66 cm (26").

No of ends: 528 (doubled at the edges).

Weft

Cottolin 22/2, dark brick-red, 160 g (5.6 oz).

Weaving

Approx. 9 picks per cm (22.5 ppi).

The hem is woven in this way: 1.5 cm (0.6") plain weave + 1½ repeats of pattern + 8 picks of plain weave. (See *Remarks*).

12 cm (5") pattern

Border: 9 picks of plain weave + 2½ repeats of pattern + 9 picks of plain weave.

90 cm (35") pattern

Repeat border + 12 cm (5") pattern + hem.

Remarks

This weave has a considerable take-up. Areas of plain wave will not shrink in the same way, as can be seen from the two plain weave bands of the border. They show a seersucker effect. So even if it is very easy to put a plain weave border along the selvages, and weave all plain weave for the seam allowance, it is not recommended. To prevent the hem from flaring in this towel, it is woven with narrow bands of pattern and plain weave (to make it flatter than all pattern).

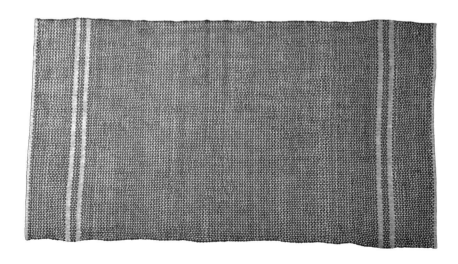

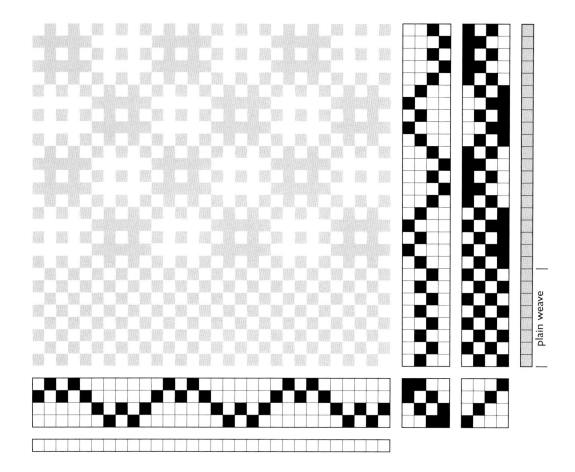

5. CHECKS AND STRIPES IN Ms-&-Os

Technique: Ms-&-Os
Finished size: see below.
Warp: Cotton 8/2, white, 62 g (2.2 oz) per towel, plus 6 g (0.2 oz) of each of these
                three colours: green, bluegreen, and turquoise.
Sett: 8 ends per cm (20 epi).
Width in reed: 55 cm (22").
No of ends: 444 (the first 2 and the last 2 ends = floating selvage, not shown on drawdown).

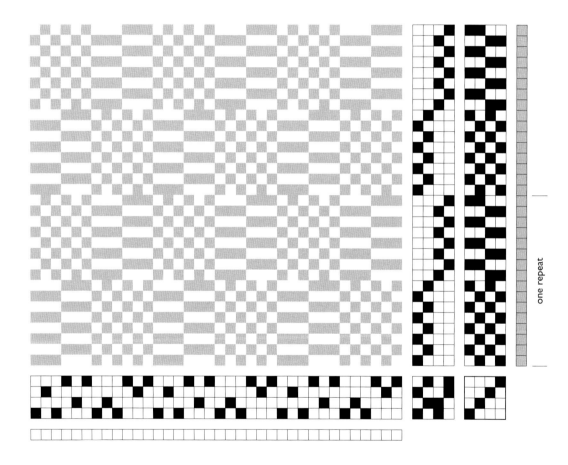

one repeat

White		30	12	12	228	12	12	30
Green			18					18
Bluegreen				18			18	
Turquoise					18	18		

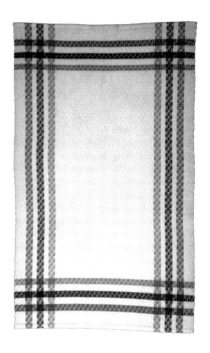

Checks

Finished size: 72 cm x 44 cm (28.5" x 17.5").

Weft: Cotton 8/2, white, 60 g (2 oz), and 6 g (0.2 oz) of each colour, per towel.

Weaving

4 repeats with white (half of this will be used for hem). 1 repeat = 16 picks = 1.8 cm (0.7").

Border: 1 repeat green + 1 repeat white + 1 repeat bluegreen + 1 repeat white + 1 repeat turquoise

50 cm (20") with white

Weave border in opposite order.

End with 4 repeats of white.

Stripes

Finished size: 71 cm x 42 cm (28" x 16.5").

Weft: Cottolin 22/2, natural, 60 g (2 oz) per towel.

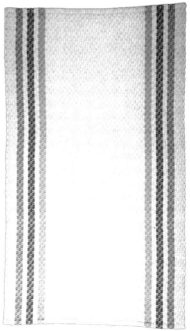

Weaving

Woven as yardage, in one long piece, and cut up afterwards. 9 picks per cm (22.5 ppi).

Remarks

The originals were woven in a cotton yarn that is no longer available. I have rewritten the instructions for cotton 8/2 and cottolin 22/2, as these yarns are universal standards.

   I have chosen not to weave a separate hem on these towels. If you would like to do so, it is easily done. See *Springtime Towels, p.24.*

6. SPRINGTIME TOWELS

Technique: Variation of Ms-&-Os
Warp: Cotton 10/2; 60 g (2 oz) per towel.
Sett: 10 ends per cm (24-25 epi).
Width in reed: 50 cm (approx. 20").
No of ends: 500 (the first 2 and the last 2 = double floating selvage, not shown on drawdown)

Green Towel

Finished size: 80 cm x 47 cm (31.5" x 18.5")
Weft: Linen 12/1 or linen 16/1, pale green; 72 g (2.5 oz) per towel.

Weaving

Approx. 10 picks per cm (25 ppi).
Begin with 5 cm (2") hem, see drawdown.
Weave the next 90 cm or so (approx. 35.5") as shown in the drawdown, alternating the two blocks of 8 picks each.
End with 5 cm (2") hem.

Turquoise Towel

Finished size: 72 cm x 46 cm (28" x 18").
Weft: Cotton 8/2 or 10/2, turquoise and white; approx. 60 g (2 oz) turquoise and 5g (0.2 oz) white per towel.

Weaving

Approx. 10 picks per cm (25 ppi).
Begin with 5 cm hem, see drawdown.
Weave A + B + A + B + A with the turquoise yarn,
change to the white yarn and weave 20 picks of twill (block B enlarged).
With turquoise: Weave A + B + A.
With white: 20 picks of twill.
Then approx. 60 cm (23.5") of turquoise, blocks A and B alternately, ending with block A,
repeat the border, and end with hem.

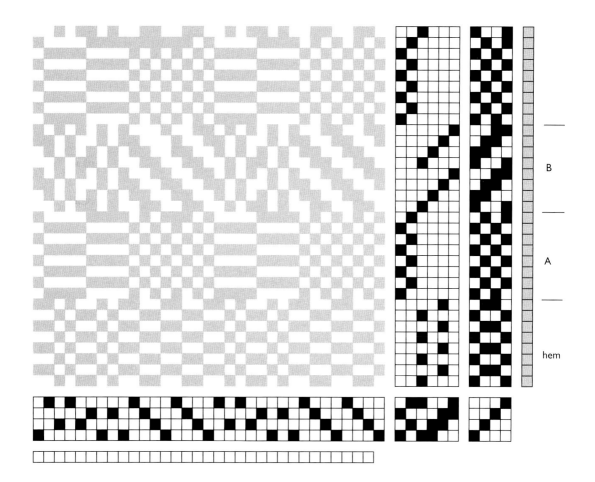

7. MOCK DAMASK

This interesting weave was presented by Gloria Martin in *Handwoven* Jan/Feb 94, as Three-end Twill Blocks. To distinguish it from the 6 shaft version (see below), one should add: 'for four shafts', but this makes it a clumsy name, so I prefer the pet name 'mock damask'.

True damask requires a minimum of 10 shafts (2 x 5 shaft satin), so this is a find for weavers with four shafts. It looks like, and can be used as, twill blocks (also known as false damask), a weave requiring a minimum of 6 shafts (2 x 3 shaft twill) and most often done on 8 shafts (2 x 4 shaft twill).

The two blocks of mock damask are front and back of a kind of twill – one block with weft effect, the other with warp effect and both with slightly broken diagonal lines. It is a one-shuttle weave, and extremely useful.

Off-white Warp

Technique: Mock damask.
Finished size: 86 cm x 49 cm (34" x 19").
Warp: Cotton 10/2, natural; 65g (2.3 oz) per towel.
Sett: 9 ends per cm (22.5 epi).
Width in reed: 55 cm (21.6").
No of ends: 500 ends (the first 2 and the last 2 ends = floating selvage, not shown on drawdown).

Blue version

Weft

Cotton 20/2, blue, used triple (except in the hem); 100 g (3.5 oz) per towel.

Weaving

5 cm (2") with cotton 20/2 (used single) for hem, see drawdown.
Change to triple weft (and approx. 10 picks per cm (25 ppi))
and weave 6xA + 4xB + 4xA + 4xB for border.
Then (19xA + 19xB) x 5 + 19xA for main part of towel.
Repeat border in opposite order, and end with hem.

White version

Weft

Tow 6/1, white, 130g (4.6 oz) per towel. (Optional: Linen 16/1, white, for hem).

Weaving

As for Blue Version above.

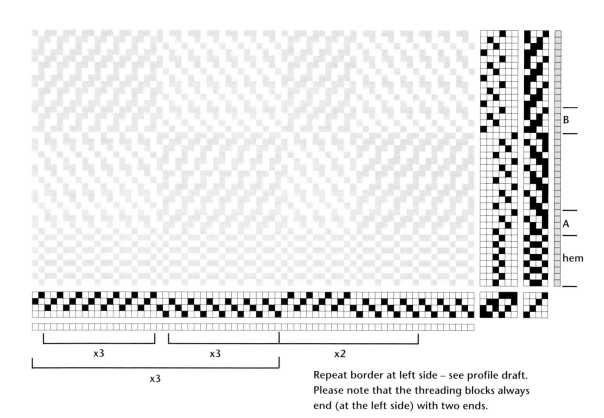

B

A

hem

x3   x3   x2

x3

Repeat border at left side – see profile draft.
Please note that the threading blocks always
end (at the left side) with two ends.

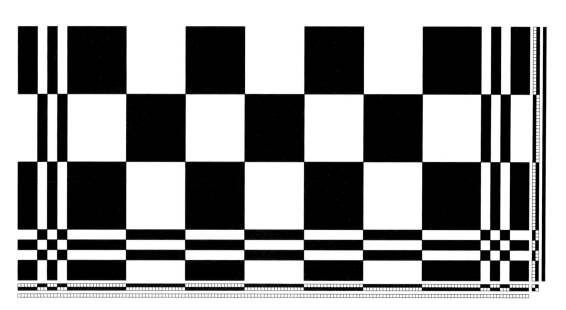

Mixed Red Warp

On the last metres of this warp I wove some Christmas placemats with a weft of dark red cottolin 22/2, which really made the red shades of the warp sparkle.

Technique:	Mock Damask
Finished size:	84 cm x 42.5 cm (33" x 16.7").
Warp:	Cotton 8/2 and/or cottolin 22/2, 4 red shades; 85 g (33.5 oz) per towel.
Sett:	8 ends per cm (20 epi).
Width in reed:	50 cm (20").
No of ends:	400 (the first 2 and the last 2 ends = floating selvage, not shown on drawdown).

The warp is made with 4 ends at a time, one of each red shade. Keep them separated while making the warp, but when threading, just take them in the order they come.

Weft
Cottolin 22/2, natural; 85 g (33.5 oz) per towel.

Weaving
Approx. 11 picks per cm (27 ppi).
Weave 3.8 cm (1.5") for hem, see drawdown,
11 cm (4.3") with the A block,
(5 x B + 5 x A) x 19 + 5 x B
11 cm (4.3") with the A block.
End with 3.8 cm (1.5") for hem as above.

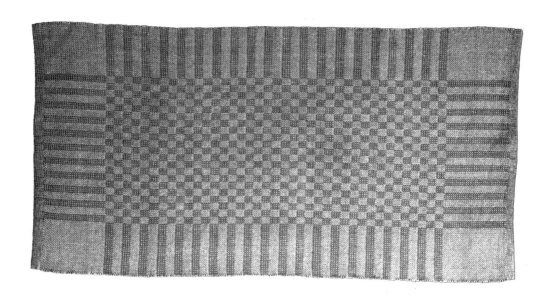

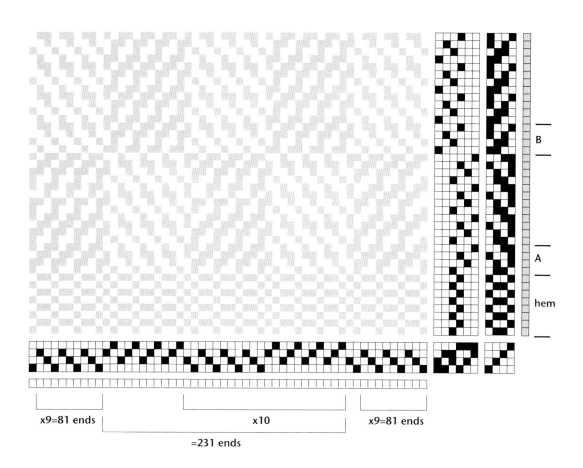

B

A

hem

x9=81 ends   x10   x9=81 ends

=231 ends

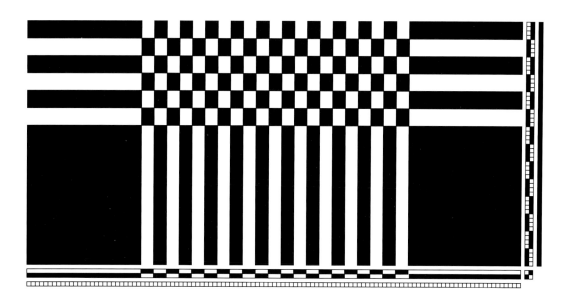

8. CHESSBOARD IN S&W

Technique: Summer-&-Winter (treadled dukagang-fashion), a two-shuttle weave where one pick of pattern is followed by one pick of tabby.

Finished size: 47 cm x 43 cm (18.5" x 17")

Warp: Cotton 10/2, natural; 35 g (1.3 oz) per towel.

Sett: 9 ends per cm (22.5 epi).

Width in reed: 50 cm (20").

No of ends: 456 (the first 2 and the last 2 ends = floating selvage, not shown on drawdown; the next 4 ends in each side double in heddle and reed = 2 x 2).

Please note that the pattern is asymmetric. The 8 x 8 squares of the towel form a useable chessboard.

Weft

Tabby: Cotton 16/2 natural; 25 g (0.9 oz) per towel.

Pattern: Cotton 20/2, red, used triple (preferably three different red shades – a nice way to use leftovers); 30 g (1.06 oz) per towel.

Weaving

First weave 4.5 cm (1.8") in tabby for hem with tabby weft.

Start weaving pattern (1 pick of pattern followed by one pick of tabby, see drawdown),

(2 x A + 2 x B) three times for border. Beat well. Ideally the tabby weft should form a balanced weave with the warp.

Main part: Weave (1 large block of A + 1 large block of B) 4 times. Make each block somewhat higher than it is wide, about 6 cm (2.4"), to make it square in the finished towel.

Repeat border, and end with hem in plain weave.

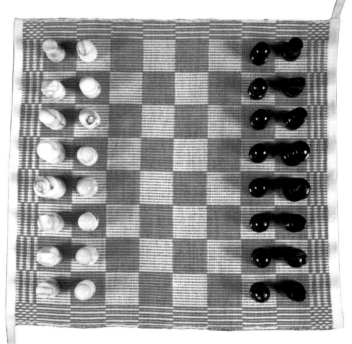

Remarks

On this almost square towel I put the 'hangers' into the end of the hem. If you don't need them, please omit them. Then the 'chessboards' can also be used as placemats.

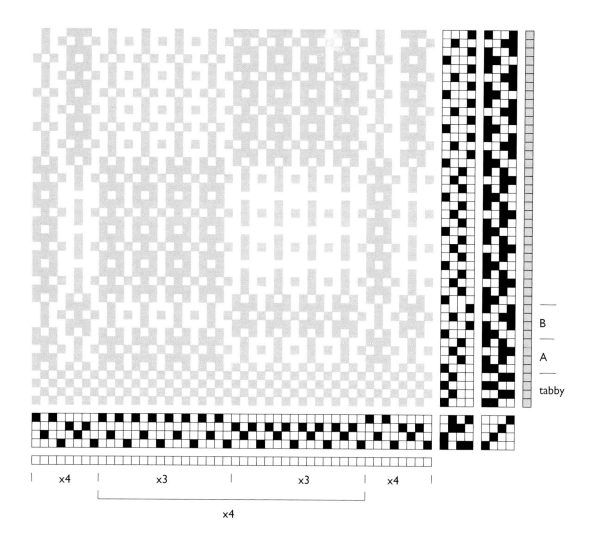

x4   x3   x3   x4

x4

B

A

tabby

Ashford Distributors

Ashford products are available from craft shops around the world. For the name of your nearest stockist contact your national distributor. If you cannot contact one of these distributors, contact Ashfords, below.

New Zealand
Ashford Handicrafts Ltd
PO Box 474, Ashburton
Tel: (64-3) 308 9087; Fax: (64-3) 308 8664
e-mail: sales@ashford.co.nz
http://www.ashford.co.nz

Australia
Ashford Australia Pty Limited
Travellers Rest, Snowy Mountains Highway
Cooma, NSW 2630
Tel: 02 6452 4422; Fax: 02 6452 4523
e-mail: ashford@snowy.net.au
http://www.ashfordaustralia.com

Austria
Wohnbauladen Alles Zum Gesunden Bauen und Wohnen
Ing Volkmar Baurecker
GoethestraBe 38, 4020 Linz
Tel: (0732) 60 22 44 0;
Fax: (0732) 60 22 44 19

Canada
Treenway Crafts Limited
501 Musgrave Road
Salt Spring Island, British Columbia V8K 1V5
Tel: (250) 653 2345 or (888) 383 7455
Fax: (250) 653 2347
e-mail: silk@treenwaysilks.com
http://www.treenwaysilks.com

Chile
Sociedad Commercial Wisniak
Louis G Salata B
Chiloe 1218 Santiago
Tel: 2 5569221; Fax: 2 5516519
e-mail losalata@interaccess.cl

Czech Republic
Dalin Praha Sro
Rezlerova 281, CZ-10900, Praha 10
Tel: 2 74860304; Fax: 2 74860304
e-mail: dinhartova@dalin-praha.cz
http://www.dalin-praha.cz

Denmark
Elsa Krogh
'Hevil', Havndalvej 40
9550 Mariager
Tel: (+45) 98 54 22 53
Fax: (+45) 98 54 26 53
e-mail: hevil@mail.tele.dk

France
Ets P Marie Saint Germain
9, rue du Capitaine, Flayelle 88203
Remiremont, Cedex
Tel: 3 29 23 00 48
Fax: 3 29 23 20 70
e-mail: annika.msg@wannado.fr

Germany
Friedrich Traub KG
Schorndorfer StraBe 18
D-73650 Winterbach
Tel: (7181) 70910; Fax: (7181) 709111
e-mail: frieder@traub-wolle.de

Japan
Ananda Co Limited
1221 Shimojyo, Nagasaka Cho
Yamanashi Pref 408
Tel: (0551) 32 4215. Fax: (0551) 32 4830
e-mail: ananda@yin.or.jp

Craft Hitsujiza
Sawaru-ku
Sohara 12-25
Fukuoka-shi 814
Tel: 92 8511 358; Fax 92 7142 962

Mariya Handicrafts Limited
Kita-1, Nishi-3, Chuo-Ku
Sapporo 060
Tel: (11) 221 3307; Fax: (11) 232 0393
e-mail: koichi-m@ra2.so-net.ne.jp

Ocean Trading Co Ltd
2F, Kyoto Toshiba Bldg
25 Hira-machi, Saiin
Ukyo-ku Kyoto
Tel: (75) 314 8720; Fax: (75) 313 6150
e-mail: ocean@alles.or.jp

Sanyo Trading Company Limited
Sanyo Building, Togashira 2-42-14
Torideshi, Ibaraki 302
Tel: 297 78 1000; Fax: 297 78 5850
e-mail: sanyo@laamies.ne.jp

Seitaro Arai & Co. Ltd
2-19-1 Akebono-cho
Naka-Ku, Yokohama 231-0057
Tel: (45) 260-3811; Fax: (45) 261 9991

Malaysia
Multifilla (M) Sdn BHD
No. 1 Jalan 2/2, Taman Industri
Selesa Jaya
Balakong, 43300S
Selangor Darul Ehsan
Tel: 3 9613686; Fax: 3 9613637
e-mail: mfilla@tm.net.my
http://www.multifilla.bigstep.com

Norway
Spinninger
Postboks 136
1361 Billingstad
Tel: 66 84 60 22; Fax: 66 84 60 22

Republic of Korea
LDH Hand Weaving Loom, Fine Corp Ltd
CPO Box 6718, Seoul
Tel: (02) 779 1894; Fax: (02) 755 1663
e-mail: finecenter@finecenter.com
http://www.finecenter.com

South Africa
Campbell Crafts & Marketing
PO Box 36180 Glosderry 7702
Cape Town
Tel/Fax 21 671 6217
email: campbellcrafts@netactive.co.za

Sweden
Gudruns Ullbod
Ulunda
745 91 Enkoping
Tel: (171) 399 95; Fax: (171) 399 96

Switzerland
Spycher-Handwerk
Gradel, Bach, 4953 Schwarzenbach b. Huttwil
Tel: (629) 62 1152; Fax: (629) 62 1160
e-mail info@spycherhandwerk.ch
http://www.spycher-handwerk.ch

Taiwan
Founder Tek Int'l Co Ltd
7F-1 177, Sec 4, Chung Hsiao East Road
Taipei, ROC
Tel: (886-2) 2781 1699/2741 9007
Fax: (886-2) 2751 2521

United Kingdom
Haldanes Craft and Tools Ltd
Gateside, Strathmiglo
Fife KY14 7ST
Tel: (1337) 860767; Fax: (1337) 868983
e-mail: haldanesltd@aol.com
http://www.spinningwheels.co.uk

United States
Crystal Palace Yarns
2320 Bissell Ave
Richmond, CA 94804
Tel: (510) 237 9988; Fax: (510) 237 9809
e-mail: cpy@straw.com
http://www.straw.com